The Feelings Book

The Care & Keeping of Your Emotions

by Dr. Lynda Madison
illustrated by Josée Masse

★ American Girl®

I get mad a lot at little things that happen.
I don't show that I'm upset, but in my room I cry.
I try to tell my family about it, but either they
don't listen or telling them makes it worse.
I don't know what to do.
Feeling Angry

Published by American Girl Publishing
Copyright © 2002, 2013 American Girl

All rights reserved. No part of this book may be used or reproduced
in any manner whatsoever without written permission except in the
case of brief quotations embodied in critical articles and reviews.

This book is not intended to replace the advice or treatment of
health-care professionals. It should be considered an additional
resource only. Questions and concerns about mental or physical
health should always be discussed with a doctor or other health-
care professional.

Questions or comments? Call 1-800-845-0005,
visit **americangirl.com**, or write to Customer Service,
American Girl, 8400 Fairway Place, Middleton, WI 53562-0497.

Printed in China
15 16 17 18 19 20 21 LEO 12 11 10 9 8 7

All American Girl marks are trademarks of American Girl.

Editorial Development: Michelle Watkins, Therese Kauchak,
Carrie Anton, Barbara Stretchberry
Art Direction and Design: Chris Lorette David, Camela DeCaire
Production: Judith Lary, Paula Moon, Tami Kepler, Kristi Tabrizi
Illustrations: Josée Masse

A Letter to You

When you were little, **your emotions were simple.** You smiled when you were happy. You cried when you were scared or hurt. You had only a few ways of responding to what happened to you, and you didn't think about your moods much at all.

Now that you're older, your emotions are more complicated. You might freeze up during a test or slam your door when you're mad. It might seem like you're on an **emotional roller coaster**—up one minute and down the next. But if you learn more about your feelings, you can keep them from racing out of control. You can be in charge—and that makes the ride a whole lot easier.

Table of Contents

How Do You Feel?

How do you feel at this very moment? **Happy? Sad? Angry? Scared?** Lots of things in your life can set off your emotions. Sometimes you will feel good . . . sometimes not so good. But all those feelings—the good, the sad, and the all-around bad—are normal. And chances are, even the happiest girl you know is sorting out her own confusing knot of emotions. So hold on and hang in there, and we'll help you figure this feelings thing out.

What Are Feelings?

"I feel great!" "I feel mad." "I feel scared!" Just what are these oceans of emotions washing over you these days?

Emotions are reactions you have to things that happen around you, and you use "feeling" words to describe them. Because the events you react to are constantly changing, it's natural that your emotions would change, too! (That's why the word "emotion" has the word "motion" built right into it.) You can be soaring to the top of the world one minute and feel stuck in the mud the next. Sometimes you may not even be sure how you feel at all.

Some days I feel happy one minute and like crying the next. I continually get mad when people ask me about my day, and I often blow up at my mom. What is happening? Why do I do this?
Confused

The better you become at identifying your feelings, the more you'll learn about yourself. People often use the words on the facing page to describe their feelings. Circle any feelings you remember having in the last week.

Elizabeth Taber Library
8 Spring Street
Marion, MA 02738

I felt . . .

thrilled   proud

shy   fearful   honored

wonderful   happy   ashamed

guilty

anxious   joyful   scared   confused

frustrated   envious

sad

annoyed   ambitious   excited

moody   embarrassed

pleased

serious   compassionate

worried   silly

brave

hopeless

sorry

loving

hopeful

giddy

respectful

careless

Your Mood-O-Meters

Each feeling you have can be strong, mild, or somewhere in between. For each situation, fill in the mood-o-meter to show where your feelings would register. If you have feelings that aren't listed here, create a new mood-o-meter.

1. You're doing homework on the computer and you accidentally delete your whole file. You feel

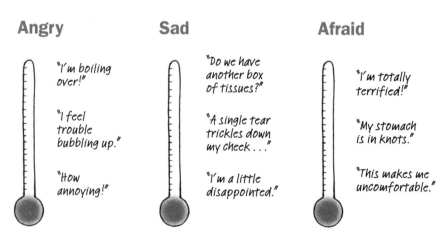

Angry

"I'm boiling over!"

"I feel trouble bubbling up."

"How annoying!"

Sad

"Do we have another box of tissues?"

"A single tear trickles down my cheek . . ."

"I'm a little disappointed."

Afraid

"I'm totally terrified!"

"My stomach is in knots."

"This makes me uncomfortable."

2. Mom announces that your family will be spending the entire summer at the beach. You feel

Happy

"Look out, ocean, here I come!"

"I'm getting excited . . ."

"I'm oh-so-satisfied."

Angry

"N-O. I won't go! N-O. I won't go!"

"Argh! I told my friends I'd sign up for summer soccer!"

"But I won't know anyone there."

Sad

"I'd call this 'super-sob sad.'"

"I'm getting teary!"

"But I'll miss my room at home."

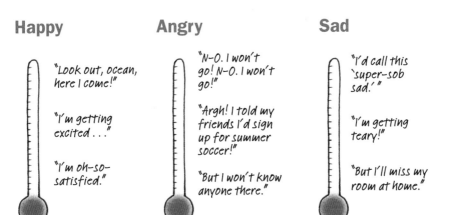

3. Someone says a friend is spreading a nasty rumor about you. You feel

Angry

ROAR!

Grrrr!

Argh!

Sad

"Waaaaah! What will I do?"

"Sniffle. I really trusted her."

"Ow. That hurts my heart."

Embarrassed

"Can I just stay home today?"

"I wish I were invisible."

"Call me Blushing Beauty."

4. You walk onto the stage to sing your solo, and you trip over the top step. You feel

Angry

"That's it! I quit!"

"Someone should have told me about that step! Who's in charge around here?"

"I knew I should have practiced my entrance."

Sad

"I can't sing when I'm crying!!"

"The reviews will call this an emotional performance."

"I wish I hadn't blown my big chance."

Embarrassed

"I wish this was a disappearing act!"

"If I trip on the way back out, maybe it will look like part of the act."

"Sheesh. I hope no one saw that!"

If you marked several mood-o-meters for any situation, congratulations! It's normal to feel more than one emotion at a time. If you weren't sure where to mark the mood-o-meters, you might not easily be flustered by your feelings. If you knew for sure, you might react strongly to some things that happen around you. But don't worry—you're going to learn how to keep feelings from boiling over.

The Brain, the Body & Butterflies

When something happens around you or to you, **your brain receives the message and tells your body systems how to react**—sometimes before you even realize it. (That's where those butterflies in your stomach come from.) Your brain works with the rest of your body as a team to help you deal with your emotions.

Brain Power

Your brain takes your feelings and makes them physical.

Your brain is in charge of everything you do, from your breathing to how you feel at any point in time. Things like movies or bad dreams aren't exciting or scary unless your brain decides they are. It gets input from everything you see, hear, feel, taste, and smell, and it responds quickly to tell your body how to react.

When I get blamed for things my little sister does, it makes me so mad that I burst into tears! After a while I cool off. Then I sit down with my parents and talk about what happened, and usually someone apologizes.
Marta, Oregon

In fact, just about every emotion you have is connected to some reaction in your body. You may blush when you're embarrassed, cry when you're sad, and jump when you're startled.

Sweaty Palms and Knocking Knees

When other parts of your body get the message that your brain is sending, they **burst into action!**

Tightening Up

When you feel tense, your muscles can get tight. You might clench your teeth, hunch up your shoulders, squint your eyes, or hold your hands in tight fists.

Feeling Butterflies

When you are stressed, your body produces chemicals that can make you feel shaky or weak. It may feel like someone is using your stomach for a trampoline. Some people call this "having the jitters" or "having butterflies in your stomach."

Sweating It

When your emotions run strong, your fore-head, armpits, hands—even the insides of your elbows—might sweat.

Knocking Knees

When you get nervous, your kneecaps may bounce up and down, especially if you're standing up. When you sit, your whole leg might bounce!

Blushing Beauty

You may get red in the face when your moods run high, especially if you're fair-skinned. But anyone's face can feel hot in reaction to strong emotions, even if it doesn't turn a few shades of red.

Ka-THUMP! Ka-THUMP!

Has your heart ever beaten so hard and fast, you thought the whole class would hear it? Strong emotions can even make you feel as though your heart were climbing up into your throat.

Casting a Dizzy Spell

Breathing too quickly can pump too much oxygen to your brain. Not breathing often enough can pump too little. Either one can leave you feeling dizzy or faint.

When you experience one of these physical reactions, don't freak out. It's normal. And it shouldn't stop you from trying new things, whether you're giving a speech, dancing in public, or saying hi to that new girl in class (imagine the emotions she must be feeling!).

Fight or Flight?

When you're upset, your heart beats faster and you start breathing more quickly. It's **your body's way of responding** to protect you.

That thumping heart is part of your body's "fight-or-flight" reaction, and it goes back to when humans first walked the earth.

Suppose you were a cave girl, just hanging out one day with your cave friends, when a fierce and hungry cave bear charged into camp. Your body's automatic responses would help you either tangle with the bear (fight) or run for your life (take flight). If you didn't do one or the other, you'd probably get eaten.

In order to fight or run away, your body would need to pump more blood to your heart (thus the pounding feeling). It would need to get your legs ready to run (thus the tight muscles). Your breathing might slow down at first so that you could be quiet and size up the situation. Then you'd probably breathe faster than normal, supplying extra oxygen to your body. You might sweat and get goose bumps in order to keep cool.

You can have a fight-or-flight reaction even when there isn't any serious danger, such as when you have to give a speech or when you hear bad news. Your body may react the same way you would have reacted as a cave girl, even though no hungry bear is sizing you up for lunch.

Why Do You Cry?

Ever laugh till your sides split? Watch a sad movie?
Goof up badly on your history test? There's a reason
any of these things can leave you in tears.

Crying is an outward sign that you feel strongly about something—usually not getting something you want or getting something you don't want. Everybody cries, even grown-ups and boys. Sometimes those tears just have to roll.

Tears serve a purpose. When you cry because of your emotions (not because of chopped onions), your tears release certain chemicals in your body. Scientists think these chemicals might actually make you feel better.

When I'm sad, I cry. Crying is a way to express your feelings. You feel better after it's all over. I also talk out loud to myself so the sadness doesn't stay as a lump in my stomach.
Katherine, Michigan

So it's OK to cry. Honest. Crying is a normal reaction to strong emotions. But some people cry so often that it becomes a problem. They get their feelings hurt easily and may think others don't like them.

Crying shouldn't replace talking about your feelings or taking actions that might help a situation. Tears just aren't the same as words. If you want people to understand what you are feeling or to know how to help, take a few deep breaths—and start talking.

Feeling Out of Control

Sometimes, before you even know what's going on, you can find yourself feeling angry, weepy, or tingly with excitement. That's parts of your body responding to your **brain releasing hormones.**

Yikes! Sometimes it seems as if you can't control your feelings. That's because feelings are often instantaneous reactions caused by your brain triggering chemicals called *hormones* that course through your body.

The *amygdala* (ah-mig-duh-luh) is a small part of your brain that scientists think is responsible for the way you feel. These two little almond-shaped groups of cells react automatically to situations that your brain thinks are funny, sad, or disturbing in some way, such as someone jumping out at you in the dark or a balloon popping. Whether you're laughing or crying at a movie or screaming as you go down a log ride at an amusement park, your amygdala is hard at work.

The *pituitary* (pi-too-i-tare-ee) is a tiny, pea-sized gland in your brain that releases hormones. Some hormones cause you to grow, while others are responsible for the changes maturing girls go through, such as starting their periods.

I've been feeling a wave of emotions lately, and I can't control it. Last week I felt grouchy and angry for no reason. But this week I've been crying a lot, even when I'm not sad. I've never felt this way before, and it's scaring me.

What's Happening Here?

As your body changes during puberty, these hormones will also start to affect how you feel emotionally. *Premenstrual syndrome* (PMS) is a group of emotional and physical symptoms that some girls—and women—experience a few days to a few weeks before their menstrual period begins each month. Hormonal changes can give you PMS and make you feel irritated or cry more easily. They can also cause headaches, tiredness, backaches, or sore breasts. Not every girl experiences PMS, and these feelings usually decrease or disappear within the first two days of your period.

What Can You Do?

The good news is that your amygdala and hormones don't act on their own. There are lots of things you can do to feel more in charge of your feelings.

Another part of your brain, the *cerebrum* (ser-ee-brum), works with the amygdala to help you manage your emotions. The cerebrum is the thinking part of your brain. Whereas the amygdala sounds the alarm, the cerebrum takes time to help you decide what to do. When you feel stressed out, let your cerebrum kick in. Try these exercises to help yourself relax and stay focused.

Take Three

You need the oxygen in the air you breathe. When you feel anxious, take a long, slow breath through your nose. Count to three as you breathe in, then hold your breath to the count of three. Now breathe out slowly, counting to three again. Repeat this three times and notice how much calmer you feel.

Flex It

When you feel tense, you may tighten your muscles without even noticing. Practice noticing how different muscles feel when they are tense, starting with your feet and moving up to your calves, rear end, back, arms, hands, shoulders, neck, and face. Hold each muscle group tightly to a count of ten, then relax. Imagine you are a pile of wet spaghetti that would just plop onto the plate if someone were to pick it up.

Use Your Imagination

Close your eyes and visualize a favorite calm, relaxing place. Feel as though you are there, with its sights and sounds and smells. Try repeating a lulling phrase to yourself, such as "Seagulls, sand, and surf."

Laugh It Up

Sometimes laughter is the best medicine. Laughing helps the brain make chemicals that stop pain and make you feel good. So laugh at silly things you do, watch a funny movie, or learn a few jokes to get your friends laughing, too.

Move It

Exercise is important for developing strong bones and muscles, and it's a great way to get your mind off things. But jogging, running, or playing a vigorous sport has also been shown to get good chemicals coursing through your brain, which can help you feel better.

Catch the Rhythm

Music can soothe or excite you, depending on its rhythm and its words. Decide what you need, and play songs that will help you relax or distract you from your troubles by getting you humming or dancing along.

Eat Right

Your brain needs the energy that comes from regular, nutritious meals in order to work well and help you solve your problems. Some people don't eat well when they are upset. Other people look to food for comfort, reaching for another cookie when they're upset. But when the cookie's gone, the problem will still be there. People who do this may gain weight and not learn real strategies for solving problems.

Stock Up on Zzzs

Your brain needs sleep to sort through what you've learned during the day and store the information. While snoozing, you're replacing chemicals your brain needs. Nine-year-olds usually need ten hours of sleep per night. Thirteen-year-olds require about nine hours. If you don't sleep enough, you will probably feel tired and grouchy during the day, and then anything that's bothering you is likely to seem even worse than it is.

Gab, Gab, Gab

Call a friend just to chat, or talk to a caring adult about how you are feeling. Sharing your concerns can make you feel better, and sometimes other people have ideas that can help.

Holding It All In

When you feel rotten, it may seem easier just to ignore the bad stuff and hope it all goes away. But a smart girl knows that's not the way to go.

When you're really upset, you may be tempted to just lie facedown on your bed and ignore the world. Even doing the things you know will help, such as exercising or talking, may seem like too much work.

But the truth is, keeping your emotions inside—especially the negative ones—only makes you feel worse. Constant stress can even increase your chances of getting sick when colds and flu bugs are going around.

Your mind can suffer, too. The more anxious you get, the more things you notice to be anxious about. You might have trouble making simple decisions, such as what to wear or what homework assignment to do first. You might get cross with people who try to help you, or give up doing things you ordinarily think are fun. The good news: you can get rid of that anxious feeling so that your emotions don't interfere with eating, learning, sleeping, and doing all the other great things waiting out there for you.

How Do You Really Feel?

When your feelings are out of control, you can't think clearly. It's smart to give yourself a chance to dig a little deeper into your emotions. **Thinking things through** helps you avoid doing or saying things you will regret later. It can help other people understand you better. And it can help you find solutions to problems you might think are unsolvable.

What's Your Reaction?

Do you blow up at the drop of a hat, or do you keep your true feelings hidden inside? For each situation, pick the reaction that is closest to the way you would probably respond.

1. You are trying to study. Your brother keeps coming into your room, messing with your games. You aren't getting anything done! You

   a. scream at him to get out—NOW!
   b. call your friend and tell her what a pain he is.
   c. clench your jaw and try to ignore him.

2. Your teacher is passing back tests and pauses at your desk. When you take the paper, a big red mark shows that you failed. You

   a. pound your fist on your desk so loudly that half the class turns around.
   b. check with other kids around you to see how they did.
   c. slide down in your chair and then slink out of class as soon as you can.

3. You open a big white envelope with your name on it and learn you won $100 in a drawing contest! You

   a. jump into the air and let out a whoop!

   b. call all the people you know and tell them the news.

   c. smile to yourself and head straight for the bank.

4. You watch a scary movie after everyone else is in bed, and then see shadowy figures in the closet every time you open your eyes. You

   a. burst out of the bedroom like a ghost is at your heels.

   b. wake your parents and tell them you can't sleep.

   c. lie there shivering for as long as it takes to go to sleep.

Answers

The Nuclear Reactor

If you had mostly **a** answers, you tend to wear your feelings on your sleeve—or anywhere else people can see them. It's great that you don't hold things in, but take care not to react too quickly and shut down communication with another person. If you immediately act angry when, underneath it all, you are actually sad, hurt, or scared, other people will get the wrong impression about how you feel. Pay attention to how your behavior affects others. You might not realize that you say or do thoughtless things that hurt the people around you.

The Talker

If you had mostly **b** answers, you let your feelings out by being chatty. Good—at least they aren't just tumbling around inside of you. Talking to others can help you sort through what you are feeling. But be careful not to speak before you think, or you could say things you regret later. Take time to think about whether you are talking to people who actually want to hear what you have to say, and make sure your words are not hurtful in some way. And don't let your chattiness keep you from figuring out how you really feel.

The Private "I"

If you had mostly **C** answers, you may be great at solving problems by yourself, on your own schedule. Or you might be a very quiet or private person who does not want to burden others with your feelings. This can be fine, as long as you don't have a storm of emotions going on inside. If you do, you'll want to get your feelings out where you can take a good look at them, so that they don't build up to the point that they make you ill. You might want to talk to others about how you feel so that they can offer help if you need it.

Put It in Your Backpack

You may not always be able to deal with your emotions right away. Sometimes it's **OK to let them rest** for a little while until you have time to deal with them.

Suppose a friend says something upsetting to you as you're going into math class, where you're about to take a test. Talking to her during class might help, but it surely would ruin everyone else's concentration. You might feel like crying or even yelling at her, but you'd embarrass yourself—and the teacher might send you to the principal's office. Sometimes you have to wait for a more appropriate time to sort out your feelings.

When we can't deal with our feelings right away, most of us stuff them into an emotional "backpack." It's tempting to leave your feelings in there, especially when your mind has moved on to something else. But if you never think about them again, your backpack could get so full that emotions spill out when you least expect it. Or you could end up carrying around so many emotions that you don't even know what's in your pack anymore. Then your health could suffer, not to mention your moods! One way or another, emotions eventually have to be dealt with.

Tip: Don't wait until bedtime to sort through confusing emotions. You might find it really hard to get some sleep. Try thinking and talking earlier in the evening and tackling just one issue at a time.

Sorting It Out

The feelings that make your backpack the heaviest **aren't always the most obvious** ones.

When you're upset, reach into your backpack and pull out the strongest feeling you're having. Then ask yourself if that's the only emotion in there, or if others are hiding there, too. You run the risk of staying just plain angry if you don't take time to discover what's really bothering you. Try these techniques to get to the bottom of things.

Keep a journal. Writing down your thoughts and feelings every day can help you sort out how you truly feel and help you solve problems. Write as though you are sharing your thoughts with a friend. You might want to keep your journal hidden from the rest of the family, but you should feel free to share it when you want to.

Fill in the blank. If you are having trouble figuring out which emotion you are feeling, try looking at the list of feelings words earlier in this book. Think about the situation that is troubling you, and use each feelings word in this sentence to see if it fits:

"I felt _____ when _____ happened."
         (feeling)   *(event)*

Talk to someone. Describing the situation can help you decide what you are feeling and can make the solution easier to see. Talking about how you feel may make you anxious or a little shy. Wait until the person can give you his or her full attention, and then say, "Can I talk to you about something I've been feeling lately?" or "Something happened today that I wondered if I could talk to you about. Do you have a minute?"

Make a "Why Else?" list. When someone says or does something that upsets you, try listing other reasons that person might have done what she did. Could she not have known it would hurt your feelings? Could she have been upset about something that didn't have anything to do with you? Her behavior could have more to do with her issues than yours, and making a "why else" list can keep you from jumping to conclusions.

Think of how others have resolved their feelings. Maybe your friend Sarah talked about her sadness and felt better. Maybe Liam hit the teacher and got expelled. Some actions help, but others can make a hard situation even worse.

Talking It Out

Sitting down with someone who cares can make you feel better and help you see your problems in a new light.

Talking to someone about your worries can help you feel less alone. You may open up to Mom or Dad, a friend, an aunt, or your best friend's mother. Whomever you choose, knowing that someone cares about you and wants you to feel better can help lighten your load.

If talking with your friends and family doesn't make you feel better, it is probably time to get professional help. Therapists, psychiatrists, and psychologists talk to you about your emotions and help you solve puzzles about why you feel and act the way you do.

A therapist talks to you (and often your parents) and helps you cope with difficult experiences. A psychiatrist is a doctor who often uses medication to treat mental and emotional disorders. A psychologist is a doctor who helps you learn to change your thoughts and behaviors.

When your thoughts or feelings interfere with the important things in life, getting help is simply the smart thing to do.

The Real World

Katie* has been upset a lot lately. A psychologist helps her understand **what's really bothering her** and what she can do to feel happier.

Katie was angry all the time. Her parents brought her to see a psychologist after she trashed her bedroom in a rage. They all agreed Katie was mad that she had come in second in the gymnastics meet the week before, instead of in her usual first place. Since then, she had been mean to her parents and testy with her sister, and she had failed a quiz in school.

Katie was nervous at first, but after spending a few minutes telling the therapist about herself, she felt a little calmer. Then she started talking about coming in second in her gymnastics meet.

Katie: I am so mad. Those judges are really dumb. I'm a better gymnast than those other girls are. I should have won.

Therapist: Are you angry because you think the judges were wrong?

Katie: Well, I'm not mad at them, I guess. It's just that I usually win.

Therapist: It sounds like you're feeling a little disappointed.

Katie: I guess so. I'm not perfect, you know. I shouldn't always have to get first place in these meets.

Therapist: Someone said you had to get first place?

Katie: Well, no. But my parents act that way. They're so proud and they brag so much when I win.

Therapist: So you think they're disappointed. It sounds like you may feel ashamed because you think you let them down.

Katie: Yes. It's really embarrassing. I'm better than that. They know it, and I know it.

There it was. Katie had acted angry. But actually, she was disappointed, embarrassed, and ashamed that she had let her parents down. Or thought she had.

The interesting thing was, once Katie talked to her parents about how she felt, she discovered they weren't disappointed in her at all! They didn't expect her to be the best all the time. They didn't even realize they were acting differently when she came in second. They were afraid that Katie would be sensitive to her loss and that it would seem insincere if they acted excited about her second-place win. All they really wanted was for her to have a good time—which she did more often once she took the pressure off herself.

*Katie's name and her interests have been changed to protect her privacy.

Strategy Session

Like Katie's feelings, yours may not always be what they seem. When you are emotional about something, **unpack your backpack** and ask the following questions:

How am I telling myself that I feel?
Fill in the blank: "I feel so _____." Your first thoughts about what you are feeling might not be correct. Or that feeling might be only a minor part of what you really feel. There could be other feelings hiding deep in your backpack, way down underneath the one that seems obvious.

Are there other feelings nagging underneath my first emotion—ones I am not even aware of?
Sometimes, underneath that feeling you think is so obvious, you can be feeling afraid, jealous, or sad. Sometimes you want and need attention and are angry when someone else doesn't see that. Take the feelings word you used above and ask yourself, "Why does this situation make me feel _____?"

What else could I be feeling?
See if another feelings word describes your emotions better. Try each one in this sentence: "Could I be feeling a little _____, too?"

Figuring out what is really in your backpack can help you truly understand yourself. Then, if you are feeling blue, you can act in a way that has the best chance of helping you feel better.

The Voice Inside

Ever think about what your thoughts say to you? Sometimes they tell you things about yourself *(I'm a pretty good artist)*, or other people *(I don't think Emma likes me)*, or even what might happen at that party tomorrow *(I don't think anyone is going to talk to me)*. **Some of your thoughts may be true, but others are definitely not.** Learning to understand and train that voice in your head can help you feel strong and confident—and deal with tough times when they come your way.

Listening In

Your inner voice usually chatters away in a pretty calm fashion. But if you're upset, your **thoughts get more emotional** and can make things seem worse than they are.

Positive Voice

When you are happy, proud, excited, or pleased, the messages you give yourself are usually positive.

Things are going really well.

Confident Voice

When you feel good, the voice in your head reminds you of things you like about yourself or of compliments others have given you. These thoughts can give you confidence to try new things and help you do well.

I know this stuff. I'm going to do well on this test.

Upset Voice

When you are sad or disappointed about something, however, your thoughts can get out of control.

I'm a loser—
a complete
failure.

When you're upset, your thoughts can turn negative and your fears can become exaggerated. Just because you flubbed your social studies test doesn't mean you're dumb. Maybe you were distracted because you stayed up too late last night. Maybe you need a new way to study. When you are angry or sad, that voice in your head may not be telling you the truth. It can call you names and tell you lies. Before you jump to conclusions, remind yourself that your negative voice may be picking up on your fears and making you feel worse.

Understanding the Circle

When you're upset, believing all the negative thoughts whizzing through your brain can make you feel worse. It can even affect how other people treat you.

It's a big circle.

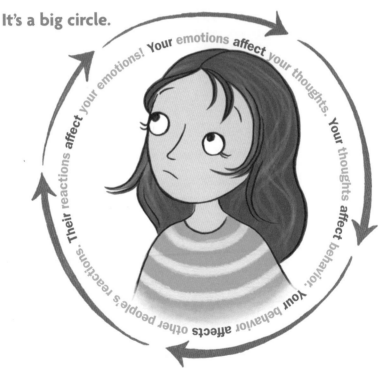

Your emotions affect your thoughts. Your thoughts affect behavior. Your behavior affects other people's reactions. Their reactions affect your emotions!

This is how many of us convince ourselves that the negative voice in our head is right. But when you believe that voice, you can become your own worst enemy. Check out the example on the next page.

Your emotions

Ellie and Leah went to the mall without me. That hurts.

affect **your thoughts about yourself,**

They don't like me anymore. They must be mad at me.

which affects **other people's reactions to your behavior.**

What's up with Alex? She must not want to hang out with us anymore. Let's just ignore her.

which affect **your behavior,**

If they're mad, I'm not going to talk to them. What's the point?

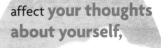

53

Changing the Circle

Changing your negative thinking can affect how others react to you—and how you feel about what is going on.

Here's how you can change a negative thought:

Stop it short. Catch those negative things you say to yourself, and hit the OFF button. Use a signal to remind yourself: clap your hands, snap a rubber band on your wrist, or even say "Stop" right out loud. Then distract yourself with another activity, such as reading or calling a friend.

Replace it. Think about possible reasons your friends might have acted the way they did. Did they not have time to call you? Did they try to call but couldn't get through? There may be lots of reasons. It's often best just to assume things are fine and go on. Remind yourself that friends can do things separately and still like each other.

Maybe they tried to call when Mom was on the phone.

Check it out. If a negative thought keeps nagging at you, find out if it's really true. Suggest an activity you and your friends can do together. If it still feels as if things aren't right, ask one of your friends privately if she's upset. Do what you can to make things right. Then forgive yourself and them—and remember that you have other friends you can do things with, too, when things are strained.

Clear Away Clouds

You're not the only person whose skies are sometimes darkened by negative thinking. But you can clear away the black clouds by learning to **question those thoughts** and work things through.

"My friend hates me."

Sometimes when you think someone dislikes you, you are actually making up how the other person feels. Before you decide this is true, consider whether something else is going on. Maybe your friend dislikes what you did, but she still likes you. Maybe you were grouchy or unfriendly to her. Talk to her to see if you can learn more. On the other hand, maybe she is worried about her own popularity and is making herself feel better by leaving you out. In that case, consider whether this person is really a good friend.

"I'm not pretty enough."

Worrying about your looks gets you nowhere. Everyone of us can find someone we think is more beautiful than we are. But physical beauty isn't everything. There are great-looking people who are unhappy and average-looking people who are funny, well-liked, and respected. Forget about your reflection and focus on being the best you can be. Be healthy and fit, have fun with your style—and have faith in yourself.

"I'm stupid."

You aren't dumb just because you didn't do your best or as well as someone else did. If you look for things you could have done differently and work at them in the future, you can succeed the next time around. Tell yourself, "This is just one situation in which I didn't do well. I'll work harder next time." Then do it!

Think Smart!

The next time the voice in your head says, "You can't do that," say, **"Yes, I can."** Match a negative thought from the left-hand column with one of the smarter statements on the right. You might find more than one that can help.

59

Who Can You Trust?

Finding someone to talk with can make your feelings easier to deal with—but you have to open up to **the right person**. Read the statements below with a friend in mind to find out how good a listener she is. The more you answer "true," the better she'd be to turn to.

1. Some people seem angry and sad all the time, but not this girl. She is warm and friendly, and not just to you. She doesn't just pretend to be nice.

true   false

2. When she asks how you're doing, she stops what she's doing and actually listens to your answers. She doesn't get distracted by other things.

true   false

3. She never makes fun of other people because of mistakes they've made or tells stories about the dumb things someone else has done. She sticks up for kids whom other people make fun of.

true   false

4. She always follows through on what she says she'll do. When she says she'll call you back, she does.

true   **false**

5. She'd never say a word about anything you told her in private—unless you told her you were going to do something dangerous. Then she'd be sure to get help from an adult.

true   **false**

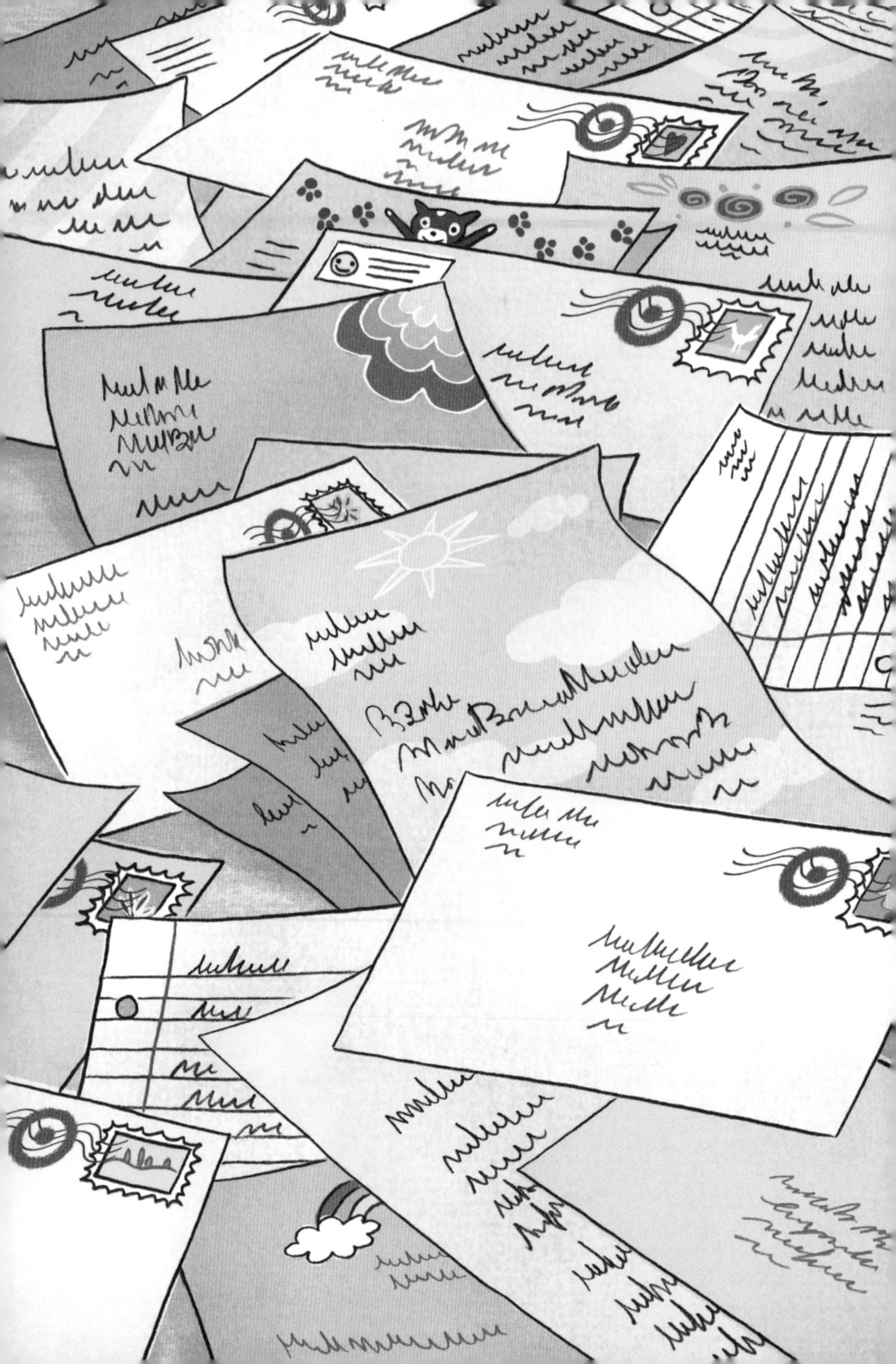

Help!

Lots of girls are dealing with confusing feelings—trying to make sense of them and learning how to cope. The big truth? No matter how you feel, you can always do something to improve a bad situation or to make a good situation better. So even when things happen in your life that you can't change, remember that **you're always in charge** of what you do about the way you feel.

I'm Scared

There are many types of fear. Some include the kind you feel at a scary movie, the kind you have when you go down into the dark basement alone, and the kind you feel when you're trying out for the soccer team. What can you do about them?

I am very scared to sleep alone at night. When I'm in bed, I imagine something will come into my room. I really want to be able to sleep alone without being afraid.

Afraid of the Dark

Put your imagination to work calming yourself down. Close your eyes and visualize a bright, cheery place. In your mind, rerun a "film" of something pleasant that happened recently—or create one about something fun coming up in your life.

If you get distracted from your imaginary movie, remind yourself that you have been lying there for several minutes—as you have for many nights in the past—and nothing bad has happened. Congratulate yourself for staying there, take a few deep breaths, close your eyes, and start up another movie. Eventually sleep will come.

When you're afraid of something that might happen but that you can't control, get the facts. Talk to your parents about your fears: "I'm worried because you two argue so much. Are you going to get a divorce?" You might find that your fears are unfounded.

If you learn they *are* getting divorced, it's OK to ask for reassurance. If you ask, "Are we going to be all right?" you'll give them a chance to remind you they will always love you. Tell them you need to know they will both stay in your life— and that you don't have to choose between them. It's OK for you to love them both.

Don't let fear stop you from trying something new. When you feel anxious about tryouts or any other new activity, ask yourself a simple question: "Then what would happen?" Here's how your mental conversation might go.

"I'm afraid of trying out for a solo. I might start singing and forget the words!"

"Then what would happen?"

"I guess I'd have to start over."

"Then what would happen?"

"Then either I'd do it better or I'd still stink."

"Then what would happen?"

"Well, I might get to sing the solo, or I'd end up just singing with the rest of the choir."

"Then what would happen?"

"I guess after a while I wouldn't be that upset, because either one would be OK."

Most likely you'll realize that you can get through the experience no matter what. Be realistic with your answers and you'll see that, slowly, your fear weakens with every "Then what?"

5. Starting middle school

4. Trying out for choir

3. Taking a big test

2. Speaking up in class

1. Saying hi to the new girl

Overcoming fear is like climbing the stairs. Each time you do something that makes you a little nervous, you take one step further from being afraid. You can conquer your fear. Don't give up!

I Feel Anxious

Sometimes you may worry that something bad could happen in the future. Sometimes you worry about something that's not likely to happen at all. Other times you feel uneasy for no particular reason. What's up?

I worry too much about whether my parents will be home when I get off the school bus. I have a list of phone numbers I can call if there's a problem, but I still worry. Can you help me?

Worrywart

Take things step by step. Make a list of situations you're afraid might happen, and with your parents' help, come up with a plan for how you'd handle each one. Then take a dry run. Ask your parents to be home but in the next room when you arrive, and walk through everything you'd do if they weren't there—make calls, ask for assistance, and so on. You'll feel calmer with them close by, and if you get stuck, they can help.

Next, practice coming home while your parents are waiting next door. If you take it one step at a time, you'll see you can handle all the scenarios on your list.

I worry about everything—tornadoes, heart attacks, all types of health problems. My mom thinks it's crazy, but I can't help it.

Caitlin, North Carolina

Between the news and crime dramas on TV, you may hear about a whole lot of scary things that can happen to people. You may feel anxious that something similar will happen to you. Some people worry a lot about events that are not very likely to occur. But worry is a feeling, not a solution.

Do a little experiment: Plan a few hours of activities with friends. During that time, stay busy. Whenever you start to worry about bad things that could happen, think "Stop!" and put your focus back on your friends and activities. When the time is up and things are just fine, congratulate yourself for not tying yourself into a worry knot!

I feel a lot of anxiety about school. My parents expect a lot from me. When I got a bad grade in math, they were disappointed—and so was I. What can I do to not stress out so much about schoolwork?

Laura, Illinois

Your parents might be disappointed with grades that are not as good as they know you could get, but that doesn't mean they don't love you. Even when they seem frustrated, their love for you is so strong that it can't be shaken by something like a bad grade. They may be angry at the situation, but they care deeply about you—don't forget that.

But there are things you can do to reduce your anxiety. If you can't fall asleep at night because you're worried about the test on Friday, don't lie there tossing and turning. Ask yourself this question: *Is there anything I can do right now to solve this problem?* Then think it through.

Is there anything I can do right now to solve this problem?
Yes. I can get up and figure out how much time I have to study and how many chapters I need to review.
No way. It's 11 p.m.! I need to sleep.
You've looked at your schedule and made your list. Is there anything else you can do now?
I'll come up with a plan first thing tomorrow.
Yes. I could start studying right now! But it's so late that I'll be exhausted tomorrow if I do.
No. It's too late.
Let it go. You've done all you can do for now.
Let it go. You have a plan and you've done all you can do for now.

I'm So Jealous

They don't call jealousy the green-eyed monster for nothing. When other people get more attention than you do, it can feel as if a beast has taken hold of you and turned you into someone you don't even know!

My friend is a really good gymnast. She can do three kinds of splits and all sorts of cool stuff. I thought I was good until I saw her. What should I do about the way I feel?

Charisse, New York

If you think about it, you wouldn't want your friend to do less than her very best. When she does a great stunt on the beam or an impressive tumbling run, try to congratulate her with a smile that's genuine.

If you can't shake your feelings of jealousy, you might need to have a serious talk with yourself. You are a worthwhile person even if you don't measure up to your friend's accomplishments. Remind yourself that you don't have to be perfect to enjoy your sport. You can also set a goal for improving your own skills—but work toward that goal for yourself, not to get the approval of others. Keep practicing, and be sure to pat yourself on the back for working so hard.

My little sister is in my cousin's wedding and I'm not. I'm really mad and a little envious. I know my cousin won't change the wedding plans for me. I wrote him a letter and I haven't heard back. I also talked to my parents but no luck there, either.

Left Out

You did the right thing by trying to communicate with your cousin about the situation. Now the ball is in his court. If he doesn't get back to you, this may be one situation you just have to accept as gracefully as you can.

That doesn't have to stop you from having a good time at the wedding, though. Get involved in the festivities rather than slinking away feeling angry and hurt. Ask if there are ways you can be helpful, such as by managing the guest book or handing out rice. Or dance your heart out at the reception. Tell yourself that your day will come—and be happy for your sister.

I've Been Disrespected

Being picked on, teased, or bullied can really hurt. But you can learn how to respond and keep your self-respect.

The girls in my class are mean and play tricks on me. They think it's funny to hurt my feelings. What should I do? This has been happening to me for years, and I am getting sick of it!

Fed Up and Hurt

Being picked on can really hurt. To stand up for yourself, you need to state the problem, say you want it to stop, and do so in a way that lets you be on good terms with that person.

It'll take some guts. When someone teases you, take a deep breath and state exactly what you don't like. Practice your words beforehand. They can be as simple as, "It really hurts my feelings when you play tricks on me." Tell her what you want: "I want you to stop."

Talk to the bully in a way that can help you be on good terms. You might try, "It's not OK with me when you say mean things. I'd like to find a way for us to get along."

If the bully doesn't stop, you will at least have shown her—and those around her—that you are calm, you know what you want, and you're not afraid to stand up for yourself.

People who tease others in a mean-spirited way usually are immature and trying to feel better about themselves. Other kids may join in out of fear that if they don't, they will get picked on, too.

Even in the meanest of groups, though, there usually are a few people who don't get as involved in the tormenting. Focus on one of these girls as someone you could become better friends with. Try to get to know her better. Ask your parents if you can have her over sometime. Meet with your teacher privately and see if she can make some new rules about classroom behavior—ones that reward people who are kind to others.

Some kids make fun of my clothes and say I wear unpopular brands. It really hurts me, and sometimes I cry. I don't talk to my parents about it, because my mom has her own ideas about what I should wear. What can I do to feel better?

Dressed to Distress

Sometimes the best thing you can do is not let on that your feelings are hurt. If you like the clothes you wear, act calm so that it doesn't show you're bothered.

If you'd like to change your style, try to get your mother to remember what she was like at your age. Ask her if she ever felt out of step when she was young, and see if you can compromise on a few items of clothing that would help you stand out a little less.

Remember that no matter what you wear, if you wear it as though you love it—with your head high and a smile on your face—you will look a hundred times better than you would with a scowl. If you act comfortable with yourself, others may even respect you for your courage to be different.

I'm Angry

Everyone gets mad. What's important is staying in charge of how you let your angry feelings out.

I get mad a lot at little things that happen. I try to tell my family about them, but they either don't listen or telling them makes it worse. Most of the time I don't show that I'm upset, but I go to my room and cry. I don't know what to do.

Abby, North Carolina

It's frustrating when people don't seem to understand how you feel. You're taking a good first step by trying to talk with your family. Next, take a look at how you tell other people you are angry.

If you start out blaming the other person—such as, by telling your brother, "You always leave me out"—he is likely to defend himself with, "No way! I don't do that!" He might even blame you back. Try using "I statements" about how you feel ("I feel left out when you don't ask my opinion."). If you explain how you feel instead of pointing fingers, the other person is more likely to hear what you say—and that will make it easier to work out a solution.

When someone does something bad to me, all these angry emotions come pouring out and I act mean. I don't know how to stop myself.

Bonnie, Pennsylvania

If you're the kind of girl who explodes when she's angry, learn to recognize the signs that you're reaching your boiling point. Does your face get hot? Do your palms sweat? Do you start breathing fast? As soon as you feel these reactions coming on, tell yourself to stop and walk away. It's OK to say to the other person that you have to think for a minute about what just happened.

Or take a few deep breaths and count to ten. Head for your room, where you can punch or scream into a pillow. All of these tactics will help you get things under control. Then you can go back to the situation ready to discuss your feelings or move on with what needs to happen next.

In softball I get really mad if I don't play well. If I strike out, I find myself crying. I'm afraid everyone thinks I'm a bad sport. What can I do?

Maura, Alabama

Every athlete makes mistakes now and then. It's part of playing any sport. But how you react when you're down can determine whether you are a winner or a whiner. You're putting a lot of pressure on yourself to do well, and you're keeping track of everything you do wrong. Stop looking for your mistakes. Instead, at the end of the game, congratulate yourself on five things you did well ("I played hard," "I was a good sport," "I caught that fly ball," and so on). When you think about an error you made on a play, focus on what you can do to correct it next time. Visualize yourself executing the play correctly.

When you are trying as hard as you can, it's easy to forget that even the most competitive teams are playing a game that is supposed to be fun. If you aren't having fun, consider doing something else with your time.

If You Lose Your Cool

Do you need to smooth things over with someone after a blowup?
Try words like these once you have both cooled off.

I didn't like fighting with you.

I know I didn't act the best I could have.

I'm sorry that I _____ (yelled, slammed the door, called you that name).

Next time, I'll try to tell you what is bothering me before I get to that point.

It might help me stay calm if you would _____ (not point your finger, stop and listen to what I'm saying, ask how I'm feeling).

I'm Lonely

Loneliness can strike when you miss someone or when it seems as if everyone else is having more fun than you are. It can even happen when you're in a room full of people.

My parents are divorced, and I go to my dad's house every other weekend. When I am with him, I am lonely for my mom. When I'm with my mom, I'm lonely for my dad. How can I not miss them so much?

Missing Mom or Dad

It's hard being away from your mom or dad. But when you're at one parent's house, you don't have to forget about the other parent. Take a picture of your mom with you to your dad's, and arrange to call her at an agreed-upon time. The same goes for when you're visiting your mother.

Are there other emotions going on, too? Are you worried about the parent who's home without you or wondering if he or she might be worried about you? Are you concerned that your other parent's feelings might be hurt if you have too much fun? The best thing you can do is talk with your parents about your feelings and ask them to help reassure you. Then focus on enjoying the parent you are with right at that moment.

Sometimes I feel invisible. Every day on the bus my best friend sits and talks to me—until her friend Ashley gets on. Then she turns around and completely ignores me. It makes me very mad and I show it. It hurts a lot, and sometimes I want to cry.

The Invisible Girl

Quiet people often get left out of busy discussions, but that doesn't mean their friends like them any less. It's possible your friend isn't aware of what she's doing. She may even think she's dividing her time equally between you and Ashley. Talk to her alone and tell her how you feel.

Remember that your behavior can affect the way others respond to you. If you turn pouty and rude when Ashley gets on the bus, your actions tell your friends you don't want to be around them and make them less likely to want to spend time with you. Don't forget that you can talk with other kids on the bus, too. Your friend doesn't have to be your only bus buddy.

When my friends and I go bowling or do other group activities, I am always the one who is left out or who isn't talking with the group. I feel lonely, as if I don't fit in.

All by Myself

There are things you can do to get along better in a crowd. You don't have to be the life of the party, but when you feel lonely, reach out to the people around you! Find someone who isn't the center of attention to talk to. Ask her to show you how to figure the score. Ask her a question about herself. Tell her something that happened at school that day. Take orders for drinks!

Some people are just more comfortable doing things with only a few people instead of a large group. The next time you are heading for the bowling alley, plan ahead of time what you can do when you feel left out. Bring along a few snacks to share or memorize a joke to tell. You could also suggest a quieter activity that would draw the group together, such as playing a game or going out for ice cream.

I'm Really Sad

Just as you can bruise your leg or break your arm, sometimes it can feel as if your whole heart hurts. And when hopeless feelings stick around longer than usual, you need to get help.

> I'm going through a lot of changes in my life, and I'm having a hard time handling all my feelings. I cry every night and I'm grumpy in the morning. I'm falling behind in my schoolwork. I don't know how to help myself.
>
> *Shea, Florida*

When you feel sad, everything in life can seem more difficult. When sadness goes too far, your mood can definitely interfere with schoolwork and relationships. That, of course, just makes you feel worse! Getting active and fighting your blue mood may be the last thing you want to do. But gather up your strength and give these ideas a try:

Get your body moving! Climb the stairs, walk the dog, or mow the lawn. Get your heart pumping!

Get outdoors for a little while, even if it's cloudy or rainy. Breathe in some of that fresh air.

Let there be light! Open the curtains and turn on some lamps. Let the light shine in.

Eat healthy food. Even if you're not hungry, try to eat three meals (or five smaller meals) a day. Stay away caffeine, such as in chocolate and certain soft drinks. Caffeine can make it hard to sleep at night, and that's the last thing you need right now.

Don't let yourself sleep in on weekends. Go to bed and get up at your usual time.

Avoid negative people. Don't spend more time than you have to with people who make you feel bad.

Don't hide, either! Make yourself say hi to others, invite someone over, or ask a friend to go to a movie.

Ask your parents to help if you are feeling overwhelmed by your chores, activities, or homework.

Draw a picture or make a sculpture of your feelings—art can help to get emotions out in front of you.

Express your sadness or anger by **writing.**

Sometimes I worry because I cry a lot. If one of my friends says something mean or if I don't get a good grade, I feel so sad. Then everything around me seems gloomy.

Down in the Dumps

When things don't go the way you wish they would, everything around you can start to look glum. It's natural that your friends are going to disappoint you once in a while and that sometimes you might disappoint yourself. It's also normal to feel sad when those things happen.

Let the sadness wash over you. Cry if you need to. Then pick yourself up and try to put whatever upset you in perspective. Make a mental list of your good qualities—you know you have them. Think about whether your not-so-great grade really means the end of the world. Then move on. In time your sadness may just go away on its own.

I've started to notice my feelings hurt a lot more. My grandmother has cancer, and I don't want to lose her. When my parents broke up, I cried myself to sleep. My grades are going down. I feel alone. I lock myself in my room and cry for hours. I need help.

Kayla, Texas

For some people, sadness gets severe and they can't shake the feeling that things are hopeless. These people may have depression. But don't get the idea that depressed people are weak or lazy. They have a serious illness, and they can get help from therapists who talk with them about their emotions and doctors who prescribe medication.

Signs of Depression

If you experience any of the feelings below, show this page to your parents and talk to them about whether a professional could help you. It doesn't always mean you have depression, but your sadness may be serious. Do you

- have sadness that lasts for more than two weeks?

- feel tired all the time?

- have difficulty paying attention or concentrating?

- often feel angry or irritable?

- not feel like doing things you usually enjoy?

- have frequent stomachaches or headaches?

- have bad feelings about yourself?

- think a lot about death or suicide?*

- feel that you could hurt yourself or someone else?*

*Note: No matter what you said to the rest of these items, if you said "yes" to either of the last two, tell an adult right away, and ask to talk to a psychologist or medical doctor.

I'm Grieving

It may happen when someone dies or when a friend moves away: you feel sad, angry, fearful, lonely, or a mix of painful emotions. The good news? You can let yourself be sad, learn from it, and get through it.

> My grandfather just died, and I'm very sad. Nothing will ever be normal again. When I go to my grandma's house for the holidays, Grandpa won't be sitting in the big chair at the end of the table, making everybody laugh.
>
> *Corey, Illinois*

Feeling grief can make you wonder how life will ever be fun again. No matter how much you hurt, the best thing you can do is to keep sharing with your family and friends. You need to release those sad feelings in order to move ahead with your life.

Talk to someone else who is missing your grandfather. Remember the good times you both had with him.

Honor the person who died. Don't ignore that your grandpa is gone. Start a new tradition, such as lighting a special candle for him at the holiday dinner.

Write a letter stating all the reasons you think he was wonderful. Share it with your grandma, turn it in as an essay at school, or keep it to read again later.

Make a photo album to remember the good times you had together. Or frame something special that belonged to him.

Distract yourself with things that take your mind off your sadness for a while. Go to a movie, play with friends, and even laugh. No doubt the person you are missing would want it that way.

What Happens?

There's no "right" way to grieve. You might act quiet and withdrawn, feel tense and irritable, or cry harder than you ever knew you could. You may go through all of these feelings in one week, in one day, or in one hour!

Most people go through a few typical stages when they are grieving, although they don't always experience them in the same order. At first they can't believe the loss is happening. They may ignore what is going on. Then they may get angry or scared about it, followed by feeling sad and hopeless. Finally, they learn to accept their loss and go on with their lives.

When my grandmother died, I felt really bad that I was too busy playing to even talk to her the last time I saw her.

Guilty Conscience

It is easy to feel guilty about things you did or didn't do with a loved one who has died. Maybe you didn't say "I love you" the last time you talked. Maybe you were irritated or distracted.

It's OK to have regrets about how you acted, but every time you let guilt into your head and your heart, it chips away at you. You can't rewrite the past. Admit you made a mistake, but then try to let it go. If you want, apologize to the person who died—in your journal, in a letter you write to her, or in your thoughts. Think about times you felt close to your grandma and the good times you shared. Remember that people have a way of knowing how you really feel about them. No doubt your grandmother did, too.

When a friend moves, it can feel almost as sad as a death. It's hard to imagine every day without your dearest friend—and you don't want to. Worst of all, there's nothing you can do to stop it from happening. The good thing is you can stay friends, if you're willing to work at it. Your friend will still be out there for you to talk, e-mail, and write to. She'll just be farther away.

Before she leaves, have an envelope party to make it easier to keep in touch: Put your address and a postage stamp on a stack of envelopes, and have her do the same. Exchange stacks with a promise to stick notes and pictures in the envelopes every now and then and drop them in the mail.

After she's gone, make an effort to get together with kids you don't know as well. Your best friend will always have a special place in your heart, but there's room in there for new friends, too.

I Don't Feel Safe

Watching the bad things that show up on the news and in movies leaves many girls feeling scared, even in places where they should feel safe. How do you handle it when you're worried about something happening in your life?

My dad is in the military and is going overseas for a little over a year. I'm really scared that something bad will happen to him while he's away. But I'm also worried about my mom and me being safe on our own at home.

Fearing for My Family

When something scary happens in the world, you may wonder what it would be like if it happened to you or to someone you love. Try not to spend too much time watching the news or imagining bad things happening. Instead, do some positive things, such as finding out how you can send letters or e-mails to your dad, or thinking about what you and your friends could make or collect to send to him when he is overseas to help with what he is doing.

Tell your mom if you are concerned about the two of you staying home. She can explain what she will be doing to take care of things while your dad is away. Make plans to spend extra time with your friends and other family members. And remind yourself that many, many people—from the president to the military to police officers—are doing things around the world to make sure you and the people you love stay secure.

> I worry about school shootings. Once a boy brought a gun to my school. He was caught before anybody was hurt, but it was scary. I still don't know why it happened.
>
> *A Scared Student*

This must have been a very scary experience—one you can be sure no one wants to happen again. Knowing more about why it happened can put your mind at rest. Ask your teacher or school counselor if she can explain what went on and why the boy brought the gun. How did the teachers stop him, and what is being done now to keep people safe?

Find out who to tell if you notice anything that concerns you in the future. Talk to your parents, too. They will want to be sure you feel safe. Ask them for reassurance that they think your school is a safe place to be.

My house caught on fire last month, and I thought I was going to die. Smoke was everywhere and I was terrified. The fire trucks came and put out the fire, but everything of ours burned, even my stuffed animals. My friends have been really understanding, and we are moving to a new house soon, but I'm really afraid of that house burning down, too.

Melissa, Nebraska

You've lost a lot, and it's normal for you to be sad and a little fearful. Fortunately, you're safe and you can begin to build your life again. Although moving might make you nervous, the chances of a house fire ever happening to you again are very, very small. You can help yourself relax by making a clear safety plan wherever you live: know that there are fire alarms, what your escape route would be, and how you'd call for help.

Other kids can learn from your experience. You and your family are now experts on how to survive a house fire. Ask your teacher if you can talk with your class about making their own safety plans. People who have been through traumatic experiences often feel better when they educate others.

Your memories of the fire and what you've lost will be strong and painful, especially now. But if you stay active, keep talking to friends and family, and focus on the good things ahead of you, each day will get a little easier.

Getting Back to Normal

Right after a disaster happens, people may feel shock, fear, anger, sadness, or guilt. This is a time to be especially kind to yourself and those around you. Take care of your body and your mind, and take time to sort out your emotions. In addition to talking about your feelings, eating right, and getting enough sleep, you should try these things:

Keep a routine. Continue as many of your everyday activities as possible. Following a routine makes your world more predictable.

Turn off the TV. Watch just enough to be informed, but don't keep going over the trauma. And stay away from scary movies, too.

Talk to others who went through the disaster. Pull your family closer by talking to them and doing activities together.

Keep with a good crowd. Hang around people who are calm and don't listen to those who spread rumors.

Distract yourself a little! It's still OK to do things you enjoy and have fun with your friends.

Feeling Positive

Most of the time in your life, you'll feel pretty good about other people, the future, and yourself. But when you don't, **you'll have the skills you need** to get through the hard times—and help others get through them, too.

The Good Stuff

You've read a lot about difficult feelings such as anger, sadness, and fear. But feelings can be positive, too. Enjoy those good feelings and remember them during the rough times. (Circle) **the positive emotions** you felt last week.

I felt...

glad

hopeful

safe

optimistic

trustful

competent

able

inspired

strong

capable

proud

joyful

awed

excited

confident

grateful

happy

silly

Look Around!

Knowing how emotions work can help you understand other people and be considerate of their feelings. **How could you be most helpful** when your friends show their emotions? Circle the best answer.

1. Your good friend Noah blows up at you for losing his book. In a fit of anger, he calls you stupid and says you always mess things up. You

   a. tell him all the things he's done wrong in the past.
   b. apologize and tell him you'll buy him a new book. Mention later that you didn't think it was appropriate for him to call you a name.
   c. walk away and forget it. Who needs him for a friend, anyway?

2. Your best friend, Sophie, wins a math contest and is dancing around in the gym as if she just scored a touchdown. Other people are rolling their eyes. You

   a. decide that Sophie is terribly conceited and that you don't like her anymore.
   b. march out of the gym in a huff. Doesn't she care that you didn't even get third place?
   c. congratulate Sophie and whisper to her that she might want to calm down just a bit.

3. Trent's dog died over the weekend, but the kids at school are too busy to notice that he is sitting alone on the playground and has tears in his eyes. You

   a. yell at the other kids for not being sensitive.
   b. stay away from him because other people's sadness makes you sad, too.
   c. tell him you are sorry about his dog and let him know you care how he feels.

4. At your slumber party, you and Lauren are the only ones still awake. She confides that she's afraid and can't go to sleep. You

   a. offer to leave the light on in the hall and tell her how you visualize a peaceful scene to relax.
   b. tell her to be quiet—hey, you're trying to catch some ZZZs.
   c. wake the others and tell them Lauren's being a baby.

Answers:

If you gave the following answers, you understand that emotions can be strong and that people don't always react to them in the most positive ways. Your sensitivity makes you a great friend!

1. b. You know that Noah is just blowing off steam. You are right to offer to fix your mistake and to wait until he has cooled off to request he behave differently next time.

2. c. Sophie might not realize she is being annoying, but telling her that in an obvious way would only embarrass her and make her angry with you. Good for you for being sensitive and happy for her.

3. c. Trent is likely to appreciate your sympathy. You might even create a friendship that wasn't there before.

4. a. There's a good chance Lauren will relax once she knows she is not alone with her fear. Being sensitive to your friend's anxiety is the kind thing to do.

Keep It Up!

So, the big question: **Is it OK to feel this way?** You bet. Every experience you have, and the way you feel about it, can teach you something about yourself and help you grow. But remember, with every angry word (and with every smile) you are painting a picture of yourself in your mind—and for others to see. Be sure it's a painting you like. If you don't, now is the time to do something about it.

Take time to listen to your feelings and share them with others the best way you know how. Use the skills you learned in this book to help figure them out. If you want to learn even more, *The Feelings Book Journal* can help you sort out specific emotions and suggest things you can do about them. The better you become at understanding and expressing your feelings, the more you will enjoy being you!